ALL ALONG YOU WERE

ENOUGH

Taylor Quill

Copyright Page
© 2024 by Taylor Quill

TABLE OF CONTENTS

CHAPTER ONE

Unraveling the Stories

The Echo of Enough

I heard it softly, in the dark,
The whispers of "not good enough."
A voice I mistook for my mark,
Carved deep where skin grows soft, yet tough.

I tasted doubt upon my tongue,
The bitterness of borrowed lies.
They told me where I don't belong,
I let it seep behind my eyes.

I saw reflections in a stream,
Their waters warped my shape to none.
But still, within me lived a dream
That worth was something never won.

I feel it now, a distant song—
The truth that shakes the roots of pain.
You were enough your whole life long,
The echo still, beneath the rain.

The Scales I Cannot Carry

They placed a scale in my hands,
cold, metal-lipped and loud.
Its tongue weighed every inch of me—
every grade, every glare, every glass ceiling.

"Compare," it hissed,
its weights adorned with sharper names:
Smarter. Thinner. Better. Worthy.
Words that whistled like wind against my ears.

My fingers tasted rust, the bite of effort.
My worth was never mine, but something
served.

I held my breath and pulled the chain,
feeling the world's weight press my chest
like an anchor pressing a seabed.

But where's the scale for laughter,
for courage beneath a trembling skin?
What weighs my mother's whispered pride

or the firelight inside my veins?

There is no measure for the magic of me.
I hear it now—a silent truth like a sunrise:
I was enough before the scales.

Paper Dolls

Cut from the fabric of someone else's dreams,
I wore their stories, stitched at the seams.

Be neat, be small, don't speak, don't stray,
Fold yourself in—don't bloom, don't fray.

I felt the scissors, their careful hands,
Trimming my edges to meet their demands.

But paper tears where it bends too far,
Ink smudges on the brightest star.

I saw their eyes, a searching glow,
Chasing shadows I didn't know.

And yet my skin—beneath their glaze—
Held whispers of fire, of wilder ways.

I tore the threads that held me bound,
And heard my voice, a clearer sound.

Paper dolls can burn, can fall—
But ashes rise and sing for all.

A Room I Left for Dust

I found a small room,
filled with things I didn't need—
doubts covered in dust.

Words hung like cobwebs:
You are too much, you are less.
They clouded the light.

I brushed the walls clean.
Beneath my hands, I could feel—
soft cracks letting in air.

Here, I saw shadows
of dreams I abandoned young.
They waited for me.

I left the door wide,
letting wind sing through my chest.
I claimed back the room.

Hand-Me-Down Lies

The lies they stitched were made for me to wear,

A coat too tight with sleeves that brushed the ground.I took their weight as though they were my share.

"Be perfect," they would hum, a looping snare,
The seams of expectation pulling down.
The lies they stitched were made for me to wear.

A thousand hands, some harsh and some with care,

Threaded fears, stories never spoken loud.
I took their weight as though they were my share.

But coats like these can fray—can tear—can spare.The heart that beats beneath the whispered sound.

The lies they stitched were made for me to wear.

I peeled them off, bare shoulders kissed with air,

My worth untouched, still whole, still wholly found.

I took their weight as though they were my share,

But truth is light, and heavy threads can tear.

CHAPTER TWO

The Mirror's Truth

The Mirror's Edge

I stood before the mirror's glass,
Its silver sighs began to speak.
A girl within, both bold and brass,
And yet, her eyes looked small and weak.

She wore a voice not quite her own,
A taste of shame on every word.
A skin she'd stretched, a heart outgrown,
Yet still, she whispered, *"I'm unheard."*

The mirror laughed—a hollow sound,
And showed her frames of strangers' eyes.
The weight of wanting kept her bound,
While truth was wearing no disguise.

"You're more than fractured light and face,"
It hummed, a truth I failed to see.
The glass dissolved its rigid place—
The mirror's edge belonged to me.

Secondhand Words

I still taste them—
the secondhand words they fed me young:
"You'll never be enough."
Sharp syllables, bitter bites.

I feel them—
the silent sighs when I stumbled.
How their gaze would linger
like fingertips brushing dust.

I hear them still,
the hollow echoes of comparisons.
"Why can't you be like her?"
Her smile softer. Her voice sweeter.
Her edges clean.

I see them—
the labels stitched into my seams.
Fabric of judgment passed down,
threads of their own insecurities,
sewn into me.

But when I pause, in the quietest of quiet,
and touch the outline of my ribs,
I find room.

Room for my voice, for my hum,
and for words that feel like honey on my
tongue:
"You are not their unfinished dreams."

Her Shape in the Shadows

She stood where her shadow was long on the
wall,
A slip of herself, neither steady nor small.

The world had shaped edges too sharp to
define,

Yet whispered its ways she must follow, align.

Her face in the mirror—too soft or too square,
Her voice too much thunder, her laughter too
bare.

Each feature she mapped like a story misread,
A tale they had written but never had said.

But *listen*—the silence is clearer than sound,
It softens the edges where truths can be found.

No shadow can stretch past the light in her chest,

Where mirrors reflect how her spirit is dressed.

When I Was Nine

When I was nine, my mother said,
"Hold still, your smile's too wide."
So I pressed my lips like pages shut,
and quieted my pride.

When I was twelve, the girls would laugh,
"You're tall, too tall to dance."
So I learned to shrink my spine and hope
to miss the world's cold glance.

At seventeen, the magazines
told me what thin should mean.
So I starved my voice, my thoughts, my skin,
until I turned unseen.

The mirror kept a tally there—
each line, a silent hymn.
Its weightless glass became my judge,
its truth, a fleeting whim.

But now I see the space I took
was *always* meant to hold,
A girl with sunlit shoulders,
and a heart too loud to fold.

The Mirror Lied

The mirror lied and told me I'm too small,
A sliver of the world, a shadow's trace.
I searched for light but couldn't find it all.

It framed me still, its whispers soft and tall,
Reflections bending truth to fit my face.
The mirror lied and told me I'm too small.

Each word a scratch, a silver-fingered call—
Its edges carved my worth in empty space.
I searched for light but couldn't find it all.

It showed me frames of others, perfect, tall,
But hid my voice, my quiet, steady grace.
The mirror lied and told me I'm too small.

One day I learned to stand and watch it fall,
The glass unbroken, yet I'd found my place.
I searched for light and found it in my all.

So here I am, not hiding, not so small.
The mirror bends, but I define the space.
The mirror lied, but now—I hold it all.

CHAPTER THREE

Fractures and Fault Lines

The Beauty of Cracks

The vase lay shattered on the floor,
Each shard a song of silent pain.
But beauty bloomed where cracks once tore,
A golden seam, a healing chain.

I *felt* the sharpness of the break,
It whispered truths I'd long denied.
The pieces cut, but did not take
The heart that still refused to hide.

I *heard* the echo of my fall,
A sound both bitter, clear, and brave.
From brokenness, I stood more tall,
For strength is forged within the cave.

So let the fractures hold their grace,
Their gleam is where I start anew.
The cracks are not my fall from place,
But proof of all that I've come through.

Tasting the Ashes

Grief tastes like ashes—
burnt at the edges of dreams
you thought were fireproof.

You can *feel* it—
the phantom ache
of what was yours,
what could have been.

It lingers on your fingertips,
the memory of holding hands,
holding hope,
holding too tight.

You *see* it
in the way the sunlight hits an empty chair,
or in the shadow left behind
on a rainy afternoon.

And you *hear* it,
a whisper that crawls under doors,
"You are less without it."

But what they never tell you is this:
From ashes,
something softer grows.
Roots take hold.
And the taste of something new,
sweet and strong,
will find you.

The Fault Line's Whisper

The fault line whispered soft and low,
"This pain is not the end, you know."
The ground may break, the heart may fall,
But through the cracks, the light will call.

You *feel* the tremor in your chest,
A beating pulse that will not rest.

You *see* the scars that mark the years,
And yet they shine beyond the tears.

For broken ground still holds the seed,
And fractured hearts still learn to bleed.

The fault line speaks, a quiet song,
"In breaking, you'll become more strong."

Paper Thin

I was paper thin when you left—
a sheet, a scrap, a drifting breath.
Your words like knives, too cold, too deep,
cut edges I could never keep.

I *heard* the silence split the room,
an empty sound, a quiet tomb.
It settled heavy, like the dust,
on love turned brittle, torn by rust.

I *felt* my ribs collapse within,
a hollow space where trust had been.
My hands still trembled, reaching wide,
to hold the ghost of love denied.

And yet, in breaking, something stirred,
a voice I'd silenced, now unheard.
I folded pain into my chest,
and learned that cracks are not unrest.

I *see* the way light slips right through,
the places life had bent, not slew.
So here I stand, both soft and fierce—
A heart reborn through every pierce.

Gold in the Wounds

There's gold that gleams in every wound,
The places torn, the pieces frayed,
A brilliance earned, a life attuned.

I *feel* it hum beneath my skin,
The fault lines where I learned to fall—
Where breaking let the light seep in.

I *see* the cracks as sacred art,
Their jagged edges lined with grace,
Each scar a map of where I start.

I *hear* the quiet after storm,
The breath I thought I'd never take.
From fractures grew a softer form.

And when I taste the air again,
It's sweeter now, this gift of life.
Through breaking, I became unbent.

CHAPTER FOUR

Shedding the Masks

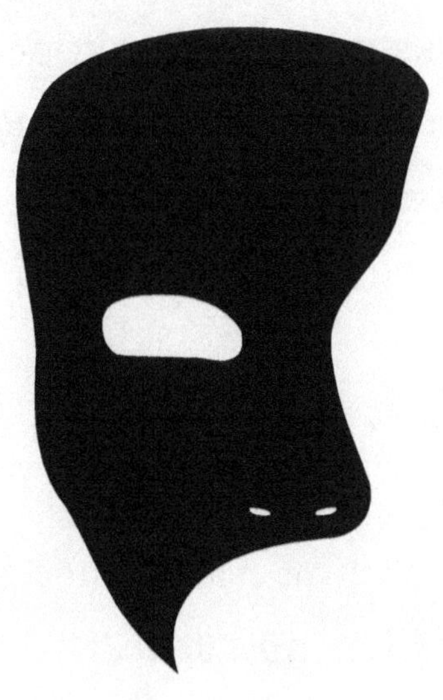

The Weight of Masks

The mask was velvet, soft and light,
It hid my face, my fractured core.
But *felt* like stone when worn too tight,
A burden I could bear no more.

I *heard* its voice, a hollow drone,
It whispered what I had to be.
A thousand roles, yet not my own,
A costume stitched invisibly.

I *saw* the cracks where light slipped in,
Its edges frayed, its threads untrue.
The mask began to shed its skin,
And all I was came into view.

I *tasted* freedom on my breath,
The air so sweet, it filled my chest.
No mask, no weight, no scripted death—
Just me, unhidden, and at rest.

Layers Unspoken

I *see* them,
the layers I've worn:
The pleaser, the quiet one,
the one who never speaks first.

I *hear* them,
their voices rehearsed:
"If you smile enough, they'll stay.
If you're small enough, you'll fit."

I *feel* them,
the layers as thick as skin.
They chafe when I walk,
pull tight when I try to breathe.

And when I *taste* the truth—
raw, unfiltered, unsweetened—
I realize this:
The world didn't hand me these layers.
I sewed them myself,
thread by thread, to belong.

But now,
I unpick the seams,
and let the layers fall
like dead leaves in autumn.
Beneath them,
there is nothing
and *everything*.
Just me.

The Painted Face

I painted my face in colors so bright,
A mask of smiles to match their delight.
I *felt* the weight of every stroke,
As truth lay quiet beneath the cloak.

I *heard* their praise, so hollow and thin,
It never reached where I'd tucked my skin.

I *saw* my reflection, a stranger's eyes,
A canvas alive with careful lies.

But the paint grew heavy, it cracked, it ran,
A river of color, betraying the plan.

So I wiped it clean, the lines and the art,
And tasted the freedom of owning my heart.

For faces unpainted may not please the crowd,
But their silence, their truth—is beautifully loud.

No Longer Small

I will not shrink, I will not fade away,
The mask has fallen, leaving only me.
A voice reclaimed will speak what it must say.

The roles I played demanded I obey,
To please, perform, and hide my wild degree.
I will not shrink, I will not fade away.

I *feel* my breath, no barriers in the way,
Each word I speak is raw and running free.
A voice reclaimed will speak what it must say.

I *see* the faces who might turn, dismay,
At truths unpolished, fierce with honesty.
I will not shrink, I will not fade away.

I *hear* my name, unfiltered and okay,
Not soft for them, but loud enough for me.
A voice reclaimed will speak what it must say.

I *taste* the life that's mine, unmasked today.
The roles are gone. I stand here, finally.
I will not shrink, I will not fade away.

Barefoot on the Stage

On a stage,
I stood in borrowed shoes—
a little too tight,
a little too polished.

The audience clapped.
I *heard* their approval like thunder.
I smiled.
I *saw* myself in a spotlight
that didn't belong to me.

Then silence.
I slipped my feet from those shoes.
The cold wood *felt* strange beneath me.
Barefoot, I walked.
The spotlight stuttered,
the applause dimmed.

And then—
a breath, a voice.
Not rehearsed. Not planned.

It *tasted* like rain on dry earth.

The real me,

barefoot on the stage,

unafraid to speak

without a script,

without a mask,

without needing them to stay.

CHAPTER FIVE

Whispers from the Quiet

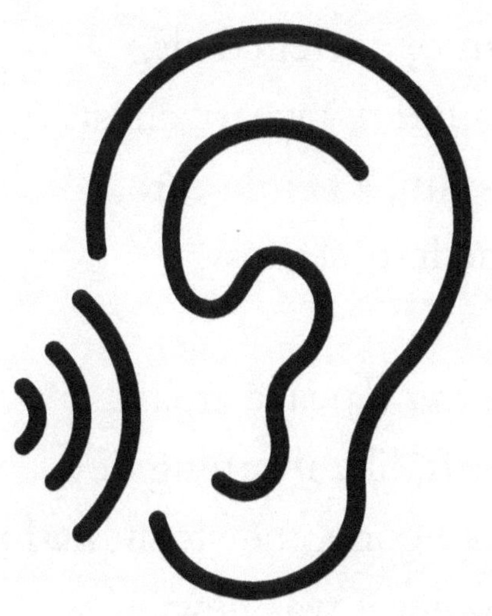

The Sound of Silence

The world grew quiet, still, and bare,
I *heard* the breath between the trees.
A whispered truth was waiting there,
A secret held on autumn's breeze.

I *saw* the light where shadows fell,
It painted gold on quiet ground.
Within the silence, calm and swell,
I found the place where I was found.

I *felt* the hum of softened air,
It curled around my weary chest.
A comfort spun, a gentle care,
To cradle me in quiet rest.

And when I *tasted* peace at last,
It lingered soft, like morning dew.
The noise had gone, the storm had passed,
And in the quiet, I was new.

The Quiet Speaks

In the quiet,
I *hear* things I could not hear before—
The soft hum of my breath,
the echo of my thoughts,
the voice I buried under noise.

In the quiet,
I *see* the shapes of my fears,
and their edges begin to soften,
like shadows at dawn.

In the quiet,
I *feel* the weight I'd carried
lift, as if the silence itself held me up.

And when I *taste* the stillness,
it is sweet.
It is slow.
It asks nothing of me,
but to listen.

In the quiet,
I discover myself—
a whisper turned song.

A Room of Stillness

I entered a room where the stillness held sway,
A soft-spoken place where the noise slipped away.

I *heard* my own heartbeat, the slowest of drums,

A rhythm untouched by the world's hurried hums.

I *felt* the soft pull of the earth 'neath my feet,
Its whisper of roots and a silence complete.

I *saw* shadows dancing, a delicate glow,
Where sunlight met walls in a slumbering flow.

And I *tasted* the air, like a memory, clean,
A sip of forgotten where I'd once been seen.

The stillness, it spoke without shouting or song,

It said, *"You were here, and you've known all along."*

Beneath the Noise

Beneath the noise, a softer voice remains,
A whisper tucked inside the quiet air.
The answers live where stillness breaks the chains.

The rush, the roar, like wild and reckless rains,
Would drown the truths I'd hidden deep in there. Beneath the noise, a softer voice remains.

I *heard* it first in gaps between refrains,
A gentle hum that I could hardly bear.
The answers live where stillness breaks the chains.

I *saw* it too—like light through windowpanes,
A glow that kissed the shadows unaware.
Beneath the noise, a softer voice remains.

I *felt* it whisper freedom through my veins,
A breath that turned to courage stripped and bare.

The answers live where stillness breaks the chains.

And now I *taste* the quiet's soft refrains,
The voice is mine, it lingers everywhere.
Beneath the noise, a softer voice remains—
The answers live where stillness breaks the chains.

The Taste of Solitude

Solitude tastes like warm tea on a cold tongue
—Bitter at first,
then soothing.

I *see* it in the slow drip of twilight,
where the sky blushes gently,
as if embarrassed by its beauty.

I *hear* it in the creak of floorboards,
in the hum of an empty room
that still holds me,
like a friend waiting.

I *feel* it settle on my shoulders,
soft as a shawl spun from quiet threads.
It carries no weight,
but it anchors me all the same.

And when the stillness folds itself around me,
I taste something I've long forgotten—
the sweetness of simply being
without needing to prove,
or earn,
or hide.

CHAPTER SIX

Seeds of Enoughness

The Seed Keeper

A single seed, so small, unseen,
Yet carries forests in its shell.
It waits for sunlight's golden sheen,
To tell it when to break its spell.

I *felt* the soil, dark, damp, and cold,
Where roots would spread to claim their place.
Though tiny hands, they still could hold
The quiet strength of time and space.

I *heard* the rain tap soft and true,
Each drop a note to wake the earth.
It whispered songs of what seeds knew:
Their worth was known before their birth.

I *saw* the sprout in emerald hue,
A fragile thing, yet fierce with might.
For in its stem, the truth rang through—
Small steps could push toward endless light.

And when I *tasted* life that grew,
The sweetness held no need to prove.
A seed becomes what it must do—
Just as I am, enough to move.

Small Steps

It begins with small steps.
I *see* the way light slips through my window,
a soft line across the floor.
Today, that is enough.

I *hear* my voice,
a whisper,
reminding me I'm here—
and still becoming.
Today, that is enough.

I *feel* the weight of my body,
how it rests,
how it rises.
Even that movement holds meaning.

I *taste* the air as I breathe it in,
each breath a promise
that something will grow.

It begins with small steps—
a seedling doesn't doubt its worth
as it reaches for the sky.
And neither should I.

Bloom Unrushed

The bloom begins unseen, below,
Where roots embrace the dark they know.

I *felt* the weight of earth's embrace,
A quiet strength, a patient space.

I *heard* the hum of water's way,
It carved through stone to find its say.

I *saw* the bud, its colors tight,
Yet held no rush to claim its light.

And when I *tasted* springtime's air,
I knew that growth is slow, but fair.

For blooms unfurl in their own time,
And worth is rooted, vast, and prime.

Enough is a Garden

Enough is a garden—
tended, not rushed.

I *feel* the soil crumble between my fingers,
soft as forgiveness.
Here, I plant small promises
of kindness,
of care.

I *hear* the hum of morning,
dew dripping from leaves,
the world whispering, *"Grow, as you are."*

I *see* green shoots rise—
uneven, uncertain,
but alive.

And when I *taste* the fruit of patience,
it is sweet.
It is mine.

Enough does not bloom in a day,
but it blooms,
always,
where love is planted.

The Roots Beneath

Beneath the earth, the roots begin to spread,
Unseen, they hold the weight of all that's grown.

We rise from ground where seeds of hope are fed.

Through storms and sun, through quiet words unsaid,

They twist and weave, though hidden and unknown. Beneath the earth, the roots begin to spread.

I *see* them in the stillness of my bed,
The dreams I sow, now sprouting seeds alone.
We rise from ground where seeds of hope are fed.

I *feel* the pull, like threads of golden thread,
That tie me to the truth I've always known.
Beneath the earth, the roots begin to spread.

I *hear* their hum, the pulse where life is led,
A steady beat beneath the soil and stone.
We rise from ground where seeds of hope are fed.

And when I *taste* the fruit from words I've said,
It proves my worth, unspoken but my own.
Beneath the earth, the roots begin to spread,
We rise from ground where seeds of hope are fed.

CHAPTER SEVEN

The Language of Loving Yourself

A Gentle Mirror

I stand before the mirror, kind,
Not searching for what's wrong.
I *feel* the strength that fills my mind,
A heart that beats so strong.

I *see* the lines, the marks of age,
Each one a story, softly told.
And in their touch, I find the sage,
A love that's pure, that's bold.

I *hear* the whispers of my soul,
A voice that sings in quiet grace.
It tells me I am whole,
I am enough, I've found my place.

And when I *taste* the air I breathe,
It's sweet with all that I have grown.
In loving me, I do believe,
This love I give is all my own.

Embrace the Imperfections

I love the curve of my body,
the softness of my belly,
the way my hands fold in their own rhythm.

I love my mind,
how it dances with questions,
how it embraces every answer,
no matter how messy.

I love my heart,
how it opens wide,
even when it has been broken.

I love the way I fall,
and rise again.
I love the way I choose me,
over and over,
without apology.

I am imperfect,
and I am complete.

A Ritual of Love

Each morning, I rise to greet my skin,
A soft embrace of love begins.

I *feel* my feet, planted on the ground,
A steady heart in every sound.

I *see* the sun through gentle glass,
A golden warmth that lets me pass.

I *hear* the breath I take with ease,
A sacred rhythm, soft as breeze.

I *taste* the quiet on my lips,
As love's embrace in me equips.

With every act, with every choice,
I speak my name, I find my voice.

Choosing Me

I choose to love the body I call mine,
With every curve and every line it shows.
I see the beauty in each shape I find.

I *feel* the strength within me, like a sign,
A power in my hands, where no doubt grows.
I choose to love the body I call mine.

I *hear* the joy that in my soul will shine,
A song that lifts me up when darkness flows.
I see the beauty in each shape I find.

I *taste* the freedom that this love defines,
A love that wraps around me as it grows.
I choose to love the body I call mine.

No more the guilt that whispers in decline,
No more the fear that stunts what love
bestows.
I see the beauty in each shape I find,
I choose to love the body I call mine.

The Heart's Affirmation

I place my hands upon my chest,
And feel the rhythm,
steady as the earth.
In this heartbeat,
I taste love
as sweet as honey on a summer day.

I *see* the scars,
the memories that have shaped me—
each one a part of my story,
etched in skin and soul.

I *hear* the whispers
of courage,
calling me to rise,
to stand in the fullness of my being.

I *feel* the warmth of self-acceptance,
like sunlight on a tender leaf.
I am enough.
I am worthy. I am love.

And in this knowing,
I find peace.

CHAPTER EIGHT

Light Between the Scars

The Map of Me

The scars upon my skin tell stories true,
Of battles fought and moments torn apart.
Each mark a map that guides me back to you,
To who I am, a work of fragile art.

I *feel* the history in every line,
A road of strength, though shadowed in the past.

These imperfections are now mine to define,
A testament to how I've made it last.

I *see* the glow that rises from the dark,
As light slips softly through the cracks I bear.
Each scar a beacon, lighting up the spark,
That grew from pain, but flourished in the air.

I *hear* the whispers of my soul's decree—
That every scar has shaped the best of me.

In the Cracks, There's Light

In the cracks of my soul, there's light.
I *feel* it,
warm as a hand held close,
gentle as a whisper against my skin.

In the places where I was broken,
I *hear* the hum of a song long sung—
the sound of healing,
soft, persistent.

I *see* the glow that spills from scars,
the light that breaks through the darkest parts,
and I know it was never in vain.

I *taste* the sweetness of survival—
the sweetness of becoming.

In the cracks,
there's always light.

Strength in the Softness

In softness lies a strength that will not break,
A tenderness that fights with quiet power.
My scars are marks of all the storms I shake.

Each wound a lesson I no longer fake,
For in the dark, I found my truest hour.
In softness lies a strength that will not break.

I *feel* the rise of courage as I wake,
A gentle flame that will not cower.
My scars are marks of all the storms I shake.

I *see* the light within each bruise I make,
A glow that blooms in every shower.
In softness lies a strength that will not break.

And when the world demands I bend or quake,
I rise, I stand, a pillar in the tower.
My scars are marks of all the storms I shake,
In softness lies a strength that will not break.

The Art of Survival

In every scar, a story waits to bloom,
A testament to strength, a broken room.

I *feel* the truth beneath each fading mark,
How darkness birthed a light that left its spark.

I *see* the beauty in the lines I wear,
Each one a reminder that I dared to care.

I *hear* the echo of resilience sing,
A voice that calls to me from everything.

And in the art of surviving, I know—
The wounds I bear are where my wisdom grows.

Wounds That Glow

The wounds that once felt sharp and cold,
Now glow with warmth and light.
They've taught me strength, they've made me bold,
bold,

To stand and face the fight.

I *feel* the power in each scar's embrace,
A softness woven deep inside.
In every mark, I find my grace,
A place where I've survived.

I *see* the radiance in the cracks,
A glow that gently spreads.
These scars are more than just the cracks,
They're signs of paths I've tread.

I *taste* the victory in my skin,
A sweetness from the past.
For all the pain that once was sin,
Has turned to light at last.

CHAPTER NINE

Returning Home to Yourself

Full Circle

I wandered far, yet here I stand,
With open arms and heart unchained.
I *feel* the warmth, a steady hand,
The peace in me, no longer strained.

I *see* the path that led me here,
Where shadows once had held me tight.
Now light fills every space, so clear,
A truth that glows within my sight.

I *hear* the whispers of my soul,
A song of love, a sweet refrain.
I'm whole again, my spirit whole,
No need to seek, no need for pain.

I *taste* the sweetness of my breath,
A freedom found in every sigh.
In coming home, I conquer death—
To self-doubt, I say goodbye.

Whole Again

I am whole again.
I *feel* the pulse of life return,
a steady rhythm in my chest.
No longer broken, no longer lost.

I *see* the pieces scattered wide,
but none were ever gone,
just waiting, like stars waiting to align.

I *hear* the quiet hum of peace,
a song that has always sung
within me, soft as breath, loud as truth.

I *taste* the air that I once feared,
now sweet with the knowing—
I am whole again.

I am enough.

The Home Within

I search no longer for a place to be,
For home was always here inside my soul.
I've found the peace that sets my spirit free.

I *feel* the warmth that comes from letting me
Be all I am, and once was, made whole.
I search no longer for a place to be.

I *see* the mirror now, and it's clear to see—
The face I thought was lost now makes me whole. I've found the peace that sets my spirit free.

No longer chasing shadows, I can see
The truth within, beyond the fear, the toll.
I search no longer for a place to be,
I've found the peace that sets my spirit free.

The Return to Self

I walked so far, through roads unknown,
But found my way, I've come back home.
The mirror now reflects my face,
A soul at peace, a heart in place.

I *feel* the softness in my skin,
A tenderness I've learned to win.
I *hear* the voice that once was lost,
Now gentle, strong, no fear to cost.

I *see* the woman that I've grown,
In every scar, in every tone.
I *taste* the sweetness of my grace,
I've come to rest in my embrace.

The Journey's End

I've come back to myself,
like a river returning to the sea.
I *feel* the calm of water's touch,
the coolness of surrender.

I *see* the shore now, vast and wide,
a place I never left, only forgot.
My body, my soul,
whole once more,
settled into the earth beneath.

I *hear* the stillness of my breath,
deep and full,
a peace that hums through every vein.

I *taste* the quiet victory,
sweet as honey on the tongue,
for I am enough.

Home is not a place—it is a knowing.
And I have returned to me.

CHAPTER TEN

All Along, You Were Enough

Always Enough

From the start, you were always whole,
A light that shimmered deep inside.
I *feel* the truth within my soul,
A power no one can divide.

You've walked through fire, yet still you stand,
With grace that no one could deny.
I *see* the strength in every hand,
The courage in your steady stride.

You are enough, this truth I *hear*,
A melody that's soft, yet bold.
I *taste* the sweetness, free from fear,
A love that's pure, a love that's gold.

In every step, you've found your way,
And all along, you've been okay.

Your Worth, Your Light

You are enough.
You are the sunrise that warms the sky,
the soft rain that heals the earth.

You are the whisper of a song,
a dance that never stops moving.

You are the heartbeat of the world,
steady and sure,
always enough.

I *feel* the power of your grace,
the strength that rises from your heart.
I *see* your light, bright as stars,
unwavering, eternal.

You are enough.
Now, and always.

Becoming You

You've always been enough, from start to end,
Your worth was there before you knew its name. Through every trial, let your spirit mend.

In darkness, you found light, a constant friend,
You danced in shadows, no one could defame.
You've always been enough, from start to end.

The scars you wear are proof you'll never bend,

A testament to all you've yet to claim.
Through every trial, let your spirit mend.

The truth is clear, no longer full of dread,
Your worth, your light, will ever be the same.
You've always been enough, from start to end.

In love, you rise, with wings that never rend,
For every step, you know you're not to blame.
Through every trial, let your spirit mend—
You've always been enough, and now, reclaim.

The Fire Within

Your fire has burned, and it still glows bright,
You were always enough, you've won the fight.

I *feel* the heat that courses through your veins,
A flame that never dies, though it remains.

You *see* the strength that rises from the ash,
A phoenix born, from every painful crash.

And now, with open arms, you rise again,
For all along, you were enough, my friend.

Celebration of You

I *taste* the victory of your love,
the sweetness of the freedom you've earned.

I *hear* the song you sing,
a melody that dances through the air,
the sound of someone who has found their way.

I *see* the glow of your spirit now,
a light that was always there,
hidden behind clouds of doubt,
shining brighter than the sun at dawn.

I *feel* the strength in your embrace,
the power of your journey in each step.
You are whole, you are worthy,
and always, always enough.

Final Note

Dear Reader,

Thank you from the bottom of my heart for picking up **All Along You Were Enough**. Every poem in this book was written with love and vulnerability, and it means the world to me that you've chosen to be part of this journey.

If you enjoyed the book, I'd be deeply grateful if you could leave a review on the platform where you purchased it. Your feedback not only helps me grow but also helps others discover the book.

And if you'd like to explore more of my writing, don't forget to check out my other books – your continued support means everything.

With gratitude,
Taylor Quill

About the Author

Taylor Quill is a contemporary poet and writer known for her evocative and heartfelt explorations of love, resilience, and personal growth. Born and raised in the Pacific Northwest, Taylor draws inspiration from the natural world and the complexities of human experience.

With a background in creative writing and psychology, Taylor's work is infused with empathy, vulnerability, and a deep understanding of the human condition. Her poetry invites readers to reflect on their own journeys, embracing the beauty and complexity of life.

Other Books From Taylor Quill

SHAPED
BY
TEA
TAYLOR

Tiny
Steps,
Big
Hearts
Poetic Moments
from the Early Years
of Motherhood
Taylor Quill